If I Were an Animal

If I Were a Sloth

By Meg Gaertner

www.littlebluehousebooks.com

Little Blue House is distributed by North Star Editions:
sales@northstareditions.com | 888-417-0195

Produced for Little Blue House by Red Line Editorial.

Photographs ©: Shutterstock Images, cover, 4, 7 (top), 18, 23, 24 (bottom left); iStockphoto, 7 (bottom), 8–9, 11, 12, 15, 17 (top), 17 (bottom), 20–21, 24 (top left), 24 (top right), 24 (bottom right)

Library of Congress Control Number: 2020913856

ISBN
978-1-64619-307-3 (hardcover)
978-1-64619-325-7 (paperback)
978-1-64619-361-5 (ebook pdf)
978-1-64619-343-1 (hosted ebook)

Printed in the United States of America
Mankato, MN
012021

About the Author

Meg Gaertner enjoys reading, writing, dancing, and being outside. No one has ever described her as slothful. She lives in Minnesota.

Table of Contents

Life in the Trees

If I were a sloth, I would live in tall trees.

I would have long claws.

My claws would help me hang on to branches. But my claws would make it hard for me to walk on the ground.

I would spend most of my life hanging upside down. I would climb down from my tree only once a week.

I would move from tree to tree using thick vines. I would move very slowly, and I would not move very far.

Eating and Staying Safe

If I were a sloth, I would

have green algae growing

on my fur.

Algae are small life-forms.

The algae would help me hide among the trees. Their colors would make me hard to spot.

I would eat mostly buds and leaves.

Eagles would like to eat me.

But I would stay safe from them in the trees.

Other Behaviors

If I were a sloth, I would

be able to swim in water.

I would use my long arms.

I would sleep many hours each day, and I would be up at night.

I would have one baby.
My baby would live on its
own after a few months.

Glossary

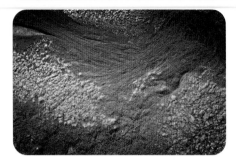

algae

eagle

claws

vines

Index

24